Alisha Ansari
2 B

The Prophets of Allah

Volume II
Elementary Level

Mildred El-Amin

Illustrated by Mike Rezac

 IQRA' International Educational Foundation

Part of a Comprehensive and Systematic Program of Islamic Studies

**An Enrichment Book
in the Program of Islamic History
Elementary Level**

Fourth Printing February 2007
Printed in China

Library of Congress Catalog Card Number 94-75982
ISBN # 1-56316-357-8

Chief Program Editors

Abidullah al-Ansari Ghazi
(PhD Harvard University)

Tasneema Ghazi
(PhD University of Minnesota)

Language Editors

Suhaib Hamid Ghazi

Huda Quraishi

Designer

Jennifer Mazzoni

(B.A. Illustration,

Columbia College Chicago)

Redesign

Sabeehuddin Khaja

IQRA'S NOTE

We, at IQRA' International Educational Foundation, are grateful to Allah ﷻ for enabling us to present the second volume of The Prophets of Allah for our young readers. The present volume contains the life and the teachings of the five prophets of Allah ﷻ (Prophet Ibrāhīm, Prophet Lūt, Prophet Ismā'īl, Prophet Ishāq and Prophet Ya'qūb) as mentioned in the Qur'an and the *Hadith*.

These books are part of IQRA's comprehensive and systematic program of Islamic education. We wish to introduce our young children to the enriched field of Islamic Social Studies through the stories and teachings of the Prophets of Allah ﷻ. This is the beginning of a comprehensive study and understanding of the role of human beings as the *Khalifah* of Allah on this planet.

The stories in this volume are incorporated in IQRA's curriculum of Islamic history (Social Studies) at first grade level. It is recommended that the teachers should consult and study the curriculum guide for daily lesson planning and teachings. However, the stories are independent enough to be read to the young non-readers in informal settings. Second and

third graders will enjoy reading these books on their own as the readability level of these stories ranges between second and third grades.

The Prophets of Allah series is the part of IQRA's comprehensive and systematic program of Islamic education which covers:

1. An integrated Curriculum from pre-school to high school.

2. A comprehensive program of Islamic studies at each level (pre-school — high school) to include ten basic Islamic subjects and to cover graded textbooks, workbooks, enrichment literature, parents'/teachers' manuals and educational aids.

We urge all concerned Muslims and Islamic organizations to co-operate with IQRA' and become an ANSAR of its educational program. We believe that together we can do it, *InshaAllah*.

Dedication

For the Glorification of Allah ﷻ alone,
we pray this book helps spark the joy of learning in young minds,
and that its inspiration is a part of the 'Ummah's unified struggle
to relieve the conditions of children around the globe!

CONTENTS

	Page
The Prophet Ibrāhīm ﷺ	3
The Prophet Lūt ﷺ	23
The Prophet Ismā'īl ﷺ	35
The Prophet Ishāq ﷺ	53
The Prophet Ya'qūb ﷺ	59

Prophet Ibrāhīm

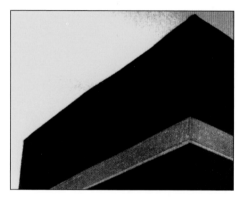

'Alaihi-s-Salātu Wa-s-Salām

YOUNG IBRĀHĪM ﷺ FINDS ALLAH ﷻ

In Mesopotamia, the country we now call Iraq, there lived a young boy named Ibrāhīm ﷺ. He did not know that Allah had chosen him for a great honor. Ibrāhīm ﷺ was to become a Prophet. The people who lived in Mesopotamia had many idols that they called gods. They did not believe in only One God, Allah ﷻ.

Ibrāhīm ﷺ was a very intelligent boy. He asked his father, Azar, "Why do you and your people take idols for gods?

The idols cannot hear and they cannot see. I know that you are wrong to worship the idols."[1] The people made the idols with their own hands from stones. Ibrāhīm ﷺ was so worried that he thought and thought, "How can I make my people see the truth?"

Ibrāhīm ﷺ knew that the idols were not Allah. Now he wanted to find the True God. When night came, Ibrāhīm ﷺ saw a star shining brightly in the sky. He said, "This must be my Lord."[2] When it set, he knew the star was not the God.

Then he saw the moon rising in beautiful splendor. It was bigger and brighter than the star. And the moon was even closer. Ibrāhīm ﷺ said, "This is my Lord," but the moon also set and then he knew the moon wasn't Allah ﷻ either. Ibrāhīm said, "If my Lord does not guide me I will be like those people who are lost."[3]

When morning came he saw the sun rising. Ibrāhīm ﷺ said, "This is my Lord! This is the greatest (light in the sky)." But at the end of the day the sun also disappeared. Finally, Ibrāhīm ﷺ knew the answer. He said, "I will no longer worship anything besides Allah."[4] Ibrāhīm ﷺ found that Allah ﷻ is the One God, Who created the stars, the moon, the sun, the earth, and everything.

Ibrāhīm ﷺ went to the market place and called to the people. He said, "Whom do you worship?" He knew that they worshipped the idols made from stones, carved into different shapes. Ibrāhīm ﷺ said, "Do the idols listen to you when you call them? Can they do you any harm or good? Allah gives me food and drink. When I am ill, Allah makes me better again."[5] The people answered, "Our fathers worshipped them." Ibrāhīm ﷺ said strongly, "You, your fathers are wrong. The idols are not God!"[6]

Even the King of that land thought that he himself was god. His name was Nimrūd. One day Ibrāhīm ﷺ told the king, "My Lord is the One God Who gives life and death." "I give life and death," said the evil king. Ibrāhīm ﷺ asked, "My God is the One Who lets the sun rise out of the east, can you make the sun rise out of the west?"[7] The King and all the people became silent. They all knew that no one can tell the sun what to do. Ibrāhīm ﷺ did not fear them. He said, "Down with you all and down with all the things that you worship. Have you no good sense?"[8]

Ibrāhīm ﷺ grew strong in faith and knowledge. He became known as the father of the Prophets and a friend of Allah.

ALLAH ﷾ PROTECTS PROPHET IBRĀHĪM ﷺ

One day when the people had gone to the big market, Ibrāhīm ﷺ took a hammer and broke all the idols except the largest one. He left the hammer hanging from the neck of that one.

When the people returned, they cried, "Who has done this to our gods?" Someone yelled, "We heard the boy called Ibrāhīm ﷺ talking bad about our idols."[9] They thought he must have done this mischief. The angry crowd marched to Azar's house and found Ibrāhīm ﷺ.

The crowd screamed at Ibrāhīm ﷺ, "Are you the one who has done this to our gods?" He said, "Ask the biggest one, see if it can tell you who broke them."[10]

They just stood there feeling ashamed. One of them answered, "You know they cannot speak or see or hear."[11] Ibrāhīm ﷺ said, "Will you worship instead of Allah that which cannot give you any harm or good."[12] Ibrāhīm ﷺ told them in a kind voice that those idols could not be God.

Nimrūd and his priests became afraid that now the people might believe in the One Almighty God Ibrāhīm ﷺ had told them about. Everyone was quiet, then one of the priests yelled to the crowd, "What will you do with the one who has destroyed your gods?" The crowd shouted, "Burn him and support your gods!"[13]

The angry crowd brought lots of sticks and made a huge pile of wood. They tied Prophet Ibrāhīm ﷺ up tight with a rope and put him in the center of the pile. He was quiet, he was not afraid because he

believed Allah was going to protect him. The people started a giant fire all around him. The fire began to sizzle and pop. Soon a black cloud of smoke came up from the fire. Everyone was sure that Prophet Ibrāhīm ﷺ would burn to death. But Allah ﷻ commanded, "O Fire be thou cool and be safe for Ibrāhīm."[14]

Everything obeys Allah ﷻ the Only God. A miracle happened! Ibrāhīm ﷺ walked out of the smoke with no harm. Allah ﷻ had protected him.

Even though the people had seen this great miracle, only a small number of them believed in the True God. Allah ﷻ told Prophet Ibrāhīm ﷺ to leave those evil people and go to the blessed land now called Palestine. Prophet Ibrāhīm ﷺ, his wife Sārah ﷺ, his nephew Lūt ﷺ and his followers left the land called Mesopotamia.

They traveled to beautiful Palestine. They began to tell the people of Palestine about Allah ﷻ and the religion of One God. Many of the people became believers in the One, Almighty Allah ﷻ.

GREAT NEWS FOR PROPHET IBRĀHĪM ﷺ

Allah ﷻ gave Prophet Ibrāhīm ﷺ the great news that he was going to have a child, who was to become a Prophet.

Prophet Ibrāhīm ﷺ and Sārah ﷢ travelled to many places and told many people about the One True God, Allah ﷻ. The King of Egypt found out that they were kind and noble people. When they were leaving Egypt, the king gave them many things. He also asked Hājar, an Egyptian lady, to go with them.

Many years passed, and still Prophet Ibrāhīm ﷺ and Sārah ﷢ had no children. He was more than eighty years old when Sārah ﷢ told him to mary Hājar ﷢ so that they may have a child.

Soon Prophet Ibrāhīm ﷺ and his wife Hājar ﷢ had a beautiful baby. They called him Ismā'īl. The baby was still very small, when Ibrāhīm ﷺ told Hājar ﷢ that Allah ﷻ had commanded him to take her and Ismā'īl ﷺ to a place called Makkah in Arabia. He was to leave them alone. Although Prophet Ibrāhīm ﷺ did not understand why, he obeyed Allah's ﷻ command. He left them in the valley of Makkah and started to go back to Palestine. Hājar ﷢ was not afraid. She

believed that Allah ﷻ was going to provide for them and keep them safe.

After Prophet Ibrāhīm ﷺ walked over the hill and could no longer see them, he turned toward the valley and prayed, "O our Lord, I have left some of my offspring to live in the valley of Makkah...fill the hearts of some people (there) with love for them and feed them with fruits so that they will give thanks."[15] Then Prophet Ibrāhīm ﷺ went back to Palestine.

In a short time all of their water was gone. The precious little baby was hungry and thirsty. He began to cry and cry. Hājar ﷺ ran back and forth between the hills Marwah and Safā, praying to Allah ﷻ for help. Right beside the baby, water flowed from the ground!

Birds saw that Allah ﷻ had provided water there and they came to drink. Soon travellers saw the birds flying over the valley and they came and settled.

Many years later, when Prophet Ibrāhīm ﷺ returned to Makkah, he found, to his surprise, that many people had come to live there. Allah ﷻ had taken care of Hājar ﷺ and Ismā'īl ﷺ, as Prophet Ibrāhīm ﷺ knew He would.

While in Makkah, Prophet Ibrāhīm ﷺ dreamt that Allah ﷻ had ordered him to sacrifice Ismā'īl ﷺ. Prophet Ibrāhīm ﷺ loved his son very much, but most of all he

wanted to please Allah ﷻ. Ismā'īl was now old enough to work with his father. Ibrāhīm ﷺ decided to tell him about the dream. He said, "O my son! I saw in a dream that I am to offer you in sacrifice." Ismā'īl ﷺ believed in the One Great God. He said, "O my father! Do what Allah ﷻ has ordered. You will find that I am patient and faithful."[16]

Father and son both wanted to obey Allah ﷻ. Isma'īl ﷺ laid face down and just as Prophet Ibrāhīm ﷺ raised up the sharp knife, he heard a voice. Allah ﷻ said, "Stop! O Ibrāhīm you obeyed the order from your dream."[17] Allah ﷻ then told him to sacrifice a lamb instead.

When Prophet Ibrāhīm ﷺ returned to Palestine, the Angel of Allah ﷻ told him that he was going to have another son named Ishāq ﷺ. Ibrāhīm ﷺ and his wife Sārah ﷺ were now very old. She said, "Shall I have a child, I am an old woman. This is indeed a wonderful thing!" Ishāq ﷺ also became a prophet.

PROPHET IBRĀHĪM ﷺ LEADS THE PEOPLE TO LOVE ALLAH ﷻ

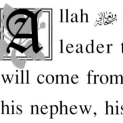llah ﷻ said, "I will make Ibrāhīm a leader to all people...and leaders will come from his family."[18] His sons and his nephew, his grandson and many of his

16

BLACK SEA
TURKEY
CASPIAN SEA
MEDITERRANEAN SEA
SYRIA
PALESTINE
IRAQ
IRAN
LIBYA
JORDAN
RED SEA
PERSIAN GULF
EGYPT
ARABIA

great grandsons would become prophets.

Prophet Ibrāhīm ﷺ sent his older son, Prophet Ismā'īl ﷺ, his younger son Prophet Ishāq ﷺ and his nephew, Prophet Lūt ﷺ to teach the people in different parts of the world. Thousands and thousands of people became believers in the religion of Allah ﷻ.

Prophet Ibrāhīm ﷺ stayed with Prophet Isma'īl ﷺ in Makkah for a long time. The two of them went to all parts of Arabia. They told people about the religion of Allah ﷻ. Many people there loved Allah ﷻ and they followed the prophets of Allah ﷻ.

BUILDING ALLAH'S ﷻ HOUSE

Allah ﷻ told Prophet Ibrāhīm ﷺ and his son Ismā'il ﷺ, "Make My Holy House for all Muslims to go around, to come for safety, and prayer."[19] Allah's ﷻ House is a holy place. It is called the Ka'bah.

Prophet Ibrāhīm ﷺ prayed that the Almighty Allah ﷻ would bless all people who obey the One Great God. He said, "Our Lord give the people a leader who would tell them about the religion of Allah ﷻ."[20] Prophet Ibrāhīm ﷺ wanted the leader to teach the people how to worship and give them wisdom.

Many years after the time of Prophet Ibrāhīm ﷺ the people began to forget the religion of Allah ﷻ. They were doing many bad things. Inside the Ka'bah they had almost 365 idols.

Two thousand years after Prophet Ibrāhīm ﷺ, Allah ﷻ sent Prophet Muhammad ﷺ to lead the people. He came from the family of Isma'īl ﷺ. Prophet Muhammad ﷺ cleaned the idols out of the Ka'bah. He told the people to obey Allah ﷻ alone and to stop doing bad things.

Prophet Muhammad ﷺ made the Ka'bah Allah's ﷻ House again. Prophet Muhammad ﷺ was Allah's ﷻ answer to Prophet Ibrahim's ﷺ prayer. He taught us Islam. All of us who follow the teachings of Prophet Muhammad ﷺ are Muslims.

Muslims come from all over the world to visit the Ka'bah. It is in Makkah, Saudi Arabia.

Millions and millions of Muslims come there every year for Hajj. They go around Allah's ﷻ House. They run between the two hills like Hājar ؓ did. They can drink from the well of Zamzam. All Muslims want to make Hajj once in their lifetime.

Prophet Lūt

a Servant of Allah

'Alaihi-s-Salātu Wa-s-Salām

FROM BABYLONIA TO PALESTINE

In Babylonia, there lived a boy named Lūt ﷺ. Babylonia was a city in Mesopotamia. The people in this city worshipped idols that they made with their own hands. They believed that those idols were gods. Lūt ﷺ, with his uncle, Prophet Ibrāhīm ﷺ, told them that there was only One God, Allah ﷻ. Lūt ﷺ was to become a prophet of Allah ﷻ.

When Lūt ﷺ learned about the One True God, Allah ﷻ, he refused to worship the idols. Lūt ﷺ was blessed to use good sense. He heard his uncle ask the people, "Why do you worship these idols? Do the idols listen to you when you call them? Can they do you any harm or good?"[21]

Lūt ﷺ thought and thought about the words of his uncle. He saw clearly that the idols had no power at all. He understood that they were not God. Lūt ﷺ began to believe in Almighty Allah ﷻ. Even though Lūt ﷺ and his uncle told the people again and again about the One True God, they did not obey. They went on worshipping the idols.

Allah ﷻ guided Lūt ﷺ and Prophet Ibrāhīm ﷺ to leave those evil people who wanted to worship idols. Lūt ﷺ said "I will leave my home for the sake of My Lord: for Allah ﷻ is Greatest in Power,

and Wisdom."22

Lūt ﷺ, along with Prophet Ibrāhīm ﷺ and his wife Sārah ﷺ and a few people from Babylonia, travelled safely to the land called Palestine. They made Palestine their new home. Palestine was a beautiful green country on the Jordan River. Many of the people there believed in Allah ﷻ, The Lord of all the worlds. Palestine was to become the homeland for many prophets.

PROPHET LŪT ﷺ
IS SENT TO SODOM

ūt ﷺ brought the message of Allah ﷻ to the people of Palestine, Syria and nearby places. His faith grew powerful and soon Allah ﷻ sent him as a prophet to the people of Sodom and Gomorrah. This was a place near the Dead Sea. Prophet Lūt ﷺ was sent to teach and to warn these people.

The People of Sodom and Gomorrah were not kind and honest. Whenever visitors came to their town, they would rob them. The people even thought it was great fun to hurt other people. They used to stop the travellers from passing on the highways. They were not ashamed to do their evil deeds right in front of everyone.

Prophet Lūt ﷺ said to them, "You are doing evil things that no other people

have ever done before."23 The people did not listen when Prophet Lūt ﷺ warned them. They were so evil that they boldly said, "Bring us the punishment of Allah ﷻ if you are telling the truth."24 "You are surely a people who do not use good sense,"25 warned Prophet Lūt ﷺ.

Those were the most sinful people. Prophet Lūt ﷺ told them, "I am a truthful Messenger sent to you. You can believe me. So fear the punishment of Allah ﷻ and obey me. I hate the things you are doing!"26 Prophet Lūt ﷺ prayed, "My Lord! save me and my family from the evil they do."27

DESTRUCTION OF THE PEOPLE OF SODOM AND GOMORRAH

The Angels of Allah ﷻ were sent to the people of Prophet Lūt ﷺ. First, they came to Prophet Ibrāhīm ﷺ and Sārah ﷺ with joyful news. They said, "Be not afraid! We bring you good news of a son who will have great wisdom."28

When they were ready to leave Prophet Ibrāhīm ﷺ asked, "What is the next thing that you have come about, O Angels (of Allah ﷻ)."29 They answered, "Lo! We are about to destroy the people of this locality (Sodom and Gomorrah). They do many wrong things."30

"O! Lūt is there!" Prophet Ibrāhīm ﷺ said painfully. They answered, "We know best who is there. Surely, we will save Lūt. Everyone in his home will be saved except his wife. She will stay with the people who refuse to obey Allah ﷻ."[31] Prophet Ibrāhīm was a gentle man. He asked, "If it pleases Allah ﷻ, will you please save the people of Lūt." The Angels replied, "The order of your Lord has been sent. They (the people of Sodom and Gomorrah) will receive a great punishment. It cannot be stopped!"[32]

The Angels came to Prophet Lūt ﷺ with the news about his people. He felt great pain and sorrow because he had no power to help them. He said, "This is a terrible day."[33]

These people were most wicked and foolish. Right in front of the Angels they did their evil deeds. "Is there not one among you who has good sense?"[34] said Prophet Lūt ﷺ.

The time of the great punishment was near. The Angels said, "O Lūt we are messengers from your Lord. Leave now! Take those in your home and leave while it is still night."[35] Prophet Lūt ﷺ and his followers had to hurry. It was almost morning. And morning was the time Allah ﷻ had set for the punishment of those who stayed behind.

The people of Prophet Lūt ﷺ dis-
obeyed all of Allah's ﷻ warnings. So

Allah ﷻ sent a storm of stones on them.

All of them were destroyed. Today, this is a place on the earth where no plants will grow. "...It is on a road that is still ruined."[36] Allah ﷻ wants us to remember what happens to evil people, who refuse to obey Him.

Allah ﷻ tells us in the Holy Qur'an, "...to Lūt, was given judgement and wisdom. He (and his followers) were saved from the people who did great evil. Lūt received Allah's ﷻ Mercy for he was one of the righteous."[37]

Prophet Ismā'īl

"Sacrifice to Allah "

'Alaihi-s-Salātu Wa-s-Salām

ISMĀ'ĪL ﷺ, A GIFT FROM ALLAH ﷻ

Baby Ismā'īl ﷺ was a precious little one. He was the first son of Prophet Ibrāhīm ﷺ. For many years his father had prayed and prayed for a child. He prayed, "O my Lord! give me a righteous child. Allah ﷻ gave him the wonderful news of a gentle son."[38] When Ismā'īl ﷺ was born, Prophet Ibrāhīm ﷺ was an old man. Ismā'īl ﷺ, like his father was to become a prophet of Allah ﷻ.

Ismā'īl ﷺ was born in the beautiful country called Palestine. It is found between the Mediterranean Sea and the Jordan River. His mother, was Hājar ﷺ. She came from Egypt which is a country on the Mediterranean Sea. She had left Egypt to serve Allah ﷻ. Prophet Ibrāhīm ﷺ married her. Hājar ﷺ and Prophet Ibrāhīm ﷺ were filled with joy when Ismā'īl ﷺ was born. The child was a gift from their Lord.

Hājar ﷺ was still nursing the baby, when Prophet Ibrāhīm ﷺ said he was going to take them on a journey. Allah ﷻ had commanded him to take them to the valley of Makkah in the desert of Arabia. Hājar ﷺ wrapped baby Ismā'īl ﷺ in a blanket and he laid quietly in her arms. She did not understand why they were leaving but she knew her husband was a friend of Allah ﷻ. And Hājar ﵁ wanted to obey Allah ﷻ.

It was a long journey from Palestine to the valley of Makkah. They travelled for many days. When they reached the valley they found it was very different place. Palestine was a beautiful green land. In the valley there were no plants, no animals and no other people to be seen. Hājar ﵁ was thankful that Allah ﷻ had given them a safe journey. She sat down to rest and to nurse her baby.

Prophet Ibrāhīm ﵇ gave Hājar ﵁ a leather bag filled with dates and a water-skin filled with water then he walked away. Carrying baby Ismā'īl ﵇, she followed him. "O Ibrāhīm! Where are you going? Are you leaving us alone in this valley?" She asked again and again. He did not answer. Then she asked, "Has Allah ﷻ ordered you to leave us here?" He said, "Yes." She said, "Then Allah ﷻ will take care of us."[39] Hājar's ﵁ faith in Allah ﷻ was strong. And she wanted to be obedient to her Allah ﷻ.

THE WELL OF ZAM-ZAM

lone in the valley, Hājar ﵁ sat and calmly nursed baby Ismā'īl ﵇. Soon there was no more water and no milk

in her breast for the baby. He was so hungry and thirsty. Ismā'īl ﷺ began to cry and cry until he was near death. Hājar ﷺ thought that she must find some water. The Help of Allah ﷻ is always near. She gently laid the baby down and began to look for help.

Hājar ﷺ ran to the top of the hill called Safā and looked all around. There were no people and no water in sight. Then she ran across the hot desert sand to the top of another hill called Marwah. She looked and looked. There was no one anywhere. Seven times she ran back and forth between the two hills. All the time Hājar ﷺ was praying to Allah ﷻ for help.

Hājar ﷺ looked back at baby Ismā'īl ﷺ and saw a miracle. Behold! an Angel of Allah ﷻ hit the earth right beside baby Isma'īl. *Allah–U–Akbar!* Water gushed up out of the sand. Hājar ﷺ ran to the water. She joyfully, gave a drink to her thirsty baby and drank herself. Then she scooped up enough water with her hands to fill her water–skin.

Hājar ﷺ was so excited to find the gushing water in the desert that she wanted to hold it and began to dig the sand up around the water to keep it from flowing over.

The cool wholesome water made Hājar ﷺ feel strong again. She had plenty

of milk in her breast for Isma'īl عليه السلام. Allah's تعالى Mercy is always near for those who obey.

Soon after some people from the tribe of Banū Jurhum were passing through the valley of Makkah. To their surprise, they saw birds flying over head. "Birds only come where there is water,"[40] they thought. So they searched for the water and found Hājar رضى الله عنها and Isma'īl عليه السلام living near the well of Zamzam.

"Will you let us live here?" they asked. "Yes, but you can never own the water. The water belongs to Allah تعالى and it is for all Allah تعالى's creatures."[41] Hājar رضى الله عنها told them. They agreed to what she said. So the people of Banū Jurhum stayed in Makkah. Hājar رضى الله عنها was glad they had come. The valley became their home. Isma'īl عليه السلام grew up with those people. They loved and admired him.

THE SACRIFICE

As the years passed, more and more people came to live in the valley. It became known as the city of Makkah in Arabia. The city grew around the well of Zamzam. Hājar رضى الله عنها and Isma'īl عليه السلام were the first people to ever live in Makkah. Hājar رضى الله عنها was a strong Muslimah who laid the foundation of the city of Makkah.

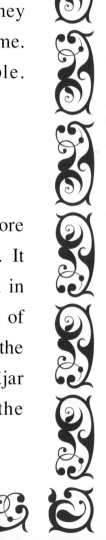

When Prophet Ibrāhīm ﷺ returned he saw Allah ﷻ had answered his prayers. He had prayed, "O my Lord...Fill the hearts of some of the people (in the valley) with love for my offspring."[42] Ismā'īl ﷺ was overjoyed to see his father. He was a gentle boy who had grown to love Allah ﷻ. Like his mother, Ismā'īl ﷺ wanted to obey Allah ﷻ.

One day Prophet Ibrāhīm ﷺ told Ismā'īl ﷺ about his dream. Allah ﷻ had given him a command in his dream. He said, "O my son! I have seen in a dream that I must give you in sacrifice. What is your thinking about this!"[43] Ismā'īl ﷺ answered quickly, "O my father! do what Allah ﷻ has commanded you. I will be, *Insha' Allah* (if Allah ﷻ wills), patient and faithful."[44]

Quietly, Ismā'īl ﷺ went with his father to a place near Makkah. He was willing to give up his life for Allah ﷻ. And Prophet Ibrāhīm ﷺ was willing to give up his only child for Allah ﷻ. They both wanted more than anything else to obey Allah ﷻ.

Ismā'īl ﷺ never became afraid. He laid down quietly with his face turned toward the ground. Just as Prophet Ibrāhīm ﷺ raised the knife, Allah ﷻ

called upon him. "O Ibrāhīm! you have already done what was commanded in your dream."[45]

Then a lamb appeared and he was ordered to sacrifice it instead. Allah ﷻ always rewards those who do right.

This was a great test. Ismā'īl عليه السلام was always faithful and patient. Allah ﷻ made him a prophet to the people of all of Arabia. Prophet Muhammad ﷺ was to come from the family of Prophet Ismā'īl عليه السلام.

BUILDING THE HOUSE OF ALLAH ﷻ

As the city of Makkah grew larger, more and more families came to live there. When Prophet Ismā'īl ﷺ became a young man, he married a woman from among the tribe of Banū Jurhum. As Allah ﷻ guided him, Prophet Ibrāhīm ﷺ came to visit his family in Makkah.

Once, when he had come to visit he found Prophet Ismā'īl ﷺ sitting near the Zamzam well. Prophet Isma'īl ﷺ joyfully stood up when he saw his father. They gave each other a long big hug. Then Prophet Ibrāhīm ﷺ gave Ismā'īl ﷺ the wonderful news. He said that they had been ordered to build the House of Allah ﷻ.

Allah's ﷻ order to Prophet Ibrāhīm ﷺ and Prophet Ismā'īl ﷺ was, "...Make My House pure for those who walk around it; for those who come there for contemplation; for those who bow there in the *Rukū'* position of prayer; and for those who take the *Sujūd* position of prayer."[46]

Prophet Ismā'īl ﷺ found many big stones for the House of Allah ﷻ. We call this House the Ka'bah. He brought the stones to his father who carefully placed each one to make the four walls of the House of Allah ﷻ. In a short time the walls became high and strong as Allah ﷻ had commanded.

49

While Prophet Ismā'īl ﷺ was handing the stones to his father, they both prayed again and again. The whole time they were building and going around the Ka'bah, they went on praying, "O our Lord accept this work from us, for You are the All–Hearing, the All–Knowing."[47]

Makkah, the home of Hājar ﷺ and her son Prophet Ismā'īl ﷺ, became a holy place for all the world. Muslims come there from all over the world to make Hajj. They circle the Ka'bah. They run between the two hills Safā and Marwah, just like Hājar ﷺ did. And they drink from the Zamzam well.

Prophet Ismā'īl ﷺ was of those who were most patient and obedient to his Lord. Allah ﷻ made him the prophet of those who believe in the One True God.

Prophet Ishāq

'Alaihi-s-Salātu Wa-s-Salām

A BLESSED MIRACLE

The birth of Ishāq ﷺ was another great thing that happened in the blessed land called Palestine. Ishāq ﷺ was the second child of Prophet Ibrāhīm ﷺ. His mother was Sārah ﷺ. This beautiful child was a gift to his parents for their good work and strong faith in Allah ﷻ. Prophet Ibrāhīm ﷺ said "Praise be to Allah ﷻ who has given me in old age (two sons) Ismā'īl and Ishāq."[48] Like his father and his brother, Ishāq ﷺ was to become one of the righteous prophets of Allah ﷻ.

Ishāq's ﷺ birth was a miracle. When he was born his parents had grown very old. Sārah ﷺ was almost ninety years old and Prophet Ibrāhīm ﷺ about one hundred years old. Sārah ﷺ had almost given up hope of having a child.

One day, some very handsome young men came to the home of Prophet Ibrāhīm ﷺ. "They said 'Peace!' He answered 'Peace!'"[49] Quickly he placed before them a table full of fine food. When the young men did not take the food, he wondered why they had refused his kindness. He began to feel some mistrust and fear of them. The young men said, "Fear not, we have been sent to the people of Lūt."[50] Now Prophet Ibrāhīm ﷺ understood, these young men were really Angels from Allah ﷻ.

The Angels also brought happy news for Prophet Ibrāhīm ﷺ and Sārah ﷻ. She laughed with joy when the Angels of Allah ﷻ said, "We give you great news of a son named Ishāq and after him a grandson named Ya'qūb."[51] Sārah ﷻ could hardly believe her ears! She had hoped for many years to have a child. She said, "Will I have a child when I am an old woman and my husband is an extremely old man? Most surely this is a wonderful thing."[52]

Prophet Ishāq ﷺ worked his whole life for Allah ﷻ. He travelled from place to place and told many people about the One True God, Allah ﷻ. From the family of Prophet Ishāq ﷺ came many prophets. From his children came Prophet Ya'qūb ﷺ, from his grandchildren came Prophet Yūsuf ﷺ. Prophets came from his great- grandchildren, his great-great-grandchildren, and for more years to come, prophets came from the family of Prophet Ishāq ﷺ. His family was highly honored and blessed. The prayers of Prophet Ibrāhīm ﷺ were answered.

Prophet Ya'qūb

'Alaihi-s-Salātu Wa-s-Salām

ALLAH'S PROMISE

One of the sons of Prophet Ishāq ﷺ was named Yaʿqūb ﷺ. Like his father and his uncle, Prophet Ismāʿīl ﷺ, he was born in the Holy Land, known now as Palestine. Palestine is the homeland of many prophets of Allah. Yaʿqūb ﷺ was the next prophet to come from his family.

Yaʿqūb ﷺ was a blessing for his grandfather Prophet Ibrāhīm ﷺ and his grandmother Sārah ﷺ. Allah ﷻ promised that many righteous leaders were going to come from this family. "Allah ﷻ bestowed on Prophet Ibrāhīm, Ishāq and Yaʿqūb, and made each of them

Prophets."[53] The promises of Allah ﷻ always come true.

Allah ﷻ blessed Prophet Ya'qūb ﷺ with a large family. He had twelve children and they were all boys. Prophet Ya'qūb ﷺ and his family lived in the land of Canaan. This place was about thirty miles from Jerusalem. On their farm, Prophet Ya'qūb ﷺ and his family had a big flock of sheep. They all worked together to care for the flock and to grow food for the family.

PROPHET YA'QŪB ﷺ LEADS HIS FAMILY

As the years passed, Prophet Ya'qūb ﷺ grew in wisdom and faith in Allah ﷻ. He taught his people about the One True God, Allah ﷻ. He taught them the same message his father and grandfather had brought to their people. Allah ﷻ made him a prophet.

Prophet Ya'qūb's ﷺ two younger sons were named Yūsuf and Benjamin. Their mother was a beautiful woman named Rahīl. One day, Prophet Ya'qūb's ﷺ son Yūsuf ﷺ came to him and told him about a special dream. Yūsuf ﷺ said, "O my father! I saw eleven stars and the sun and the moon all bow down to me."[54] At once, Prophet Ya'qūb ﷺ realized that his son's dream was the dream of a prophet and had some important meaning.

Prophet Ya'qūb ﷺ helped his dear young son to understand the dream. He said, "Thy Lord will choose you and teach the full meaning of things that will happen. Allah ﷻ will reward you and our family with great blessings. This will happen just like in the past when Allah ﷻ rewarded your great grandfather, Prophet Ibrāhīm ﷺ and your grandfather, Prophet Ishāq ﷺ."[55] Yūsuf ﷺ was to become the next prophet from this blessed family of the prophets.

Prophet Ya'qūb ﷺ lead his family and other people from his homeland to love Allah ﷻ. He said, "O my children, Allah ﷻ has given you best faith, so do not let death come to you except that you are in submission to Allah ﷻ."[56] Prophet Ya'qūb ﷺ was a kind father who guided his children to obey Allah ﷻ. When he came to the end of his life on earth, his family was near. He asked, "'Whom will you worship after I am gone?' They answered, 'We will worship the One True God, Allah ﷻ. This was the God of our forefathers, Prophet Ibrāhīm ﷺ, Prophet Ismā'īl ﷺ and Prophet Ishāq ﷺ. To Allah ﷻ we will bow in submission and obey.'"[57] A Muslim is a person that obeys Allah ﷻ; Allah ﷻ is the one who sees and hears everything.

The Prophet Ibrāhīm

1 Sūrah Al-'An'ām : 'Āyah 74 and
   Sūrah Maryam : 'Āyah 42

2 Sūrah Al-'An'ām : 'Āyah 76

3 Sūrah Al-'An'ām : 'Āyah 77

4 Sūrah Al-'An'ām : 'Āyah 78

5 Sūrah Al-Shu'arā' : 'Āyahs 70–80

6 Sūrah Al-'Anbiyā' : 'Āyah 54

7 Sūrah Al-Baqarah : 'Āyah 258

8 Sūrah An-'Anbiyā' : 'Āyah 67

9 Sūrah Al-'Anbiyā' : 'Āyahs 59, 60

10 Sūrah Al-'Anbiyā' : 'Āyahs 62, 63

11 Sūrah Al-'Anbiyā' : 'Āyah 65

12 Sūrah Al-'Anbiyā' : 'Āyah 66

13 Sūrah Al-'Anbiyā' : 'Āyah 68

14 Sūrah Al-'Anbiyā' : 'Āyah 69

15 Sūrah Ibrāhīm : 'Āyah 37

16 Sūrah Al-Ṣāffāt : 'Āyah 102

17 Sūrah Al-Ṣāffāt : 'Āyahs 104–105

18 Sūrah Al-Baqarah : 'Āyah 124

19 Sūrah Al-Baqarah : 'Āyah 125

20 Sūrah Al-Baqarah : 'Āyah 129

The Prophet Lūt

21 Sūrah Al-Shu'arā' : 'Āyahs 70–73

22 Sūrah Al-'Ankabūt : 'Āyah 26

23 Sūrah Al-'Ankabūt : 'Āyah 28

24 Sūrah Al-'Ankabūt : 'Āyah 29

25 Sūrah An-Naml : 'Āyah 55

26 Sūrah Al-Shu'arā' :
   'Āyahs 162, 163, 168

27 Sūrah Al-Shu'arā' : 'Āyah 169

28 Sūrah Al-Ḥijr : 'Āyahs 52–53

29 Sūrah Al-Ḥijr : 'Āyah 57

30 Sūrah Al-'Ankabūt : 'Āyah 31

31 Sūrah Al-'Ankabūt : 'Āyah 32

32 Sūrah Hūd : 'Āyah 76

33 Sūrah Hūd : 'Āyah 77

34 Sūrah Hūd : 'Āyah 78

35 Sūrah Hūd : 'Āyah 81

36 Sūrah Al-Ḥijr : 'Āyah 76

37 Sūrah Al-'Anbiyā' : 'Āyahs 74–75

The Prophet Ismā'īl

38 Sūrah Al-Ṣāffāt : 'Āyahs 100-101

39 Ṣaḥīḥ Al-Bukhārī – Vol IV :
    LV. The Prophets; Ch. 9

40 Ṣaḥīḥ Al-Bukhārī – Vol IV :
    LV. The Prophets; Ch.9

41 Ṣaḥīḥ Al-Bukhārī – Vol IV :
    LV. The Prophets; Ch.9

42 Sūrah Ibrāhīm : 'Āyah 37

43 Sūrah Al-Ṣāffāt : 'Āyah 102

44 Sūrah Al-Ṣāffāt : 'Āyah 102

45 Sūrah Al-Ṣāffāt : 'Āyah 105

46 Sūrah Al-Baqarah : 'Āyah 125

47 Sūrah Al-Baqarah : 'Āyah 127

The Prophet Ishāq

48 Sūrah Ibrāhīm : 'Āyah 39

49 Sūrah Hūd : 'Āyah 69

50 Sūrah Hūd : 'Āyah 70

51 Sūrah Hūd : 'Āyah 71

52 Sūrah Hūd : 'Āyah 72

The Prophet Ya'qūb

53 Sūrah Maryam : 'Āyah 49

54 Sūrah Yūsuf : 'Āyah 4

55 Sūrah Yūsuf : 'Āyah 6

56 Sūrah Al-Baqarah : 'Āyah 132

57 Sūrah Al-Baqarah : 'Āyah 133